Python Programming

Your Beginner's Guide to Learn Python in 7 Days

by

iCode Academy

© Copyright 2017 - All rights reserved

iCode Academy

The contents of this book may not be reproduced, duplicated or transmitted without direct written permission from the author.

Contents

Introduction

Python is one of the most popular of all the computer programming languages, simply because it is one of the easiest to learn. It is an all-purpose language that has a range of different applications, such as:

- Web development
- Mathematical and Scientific Computing
- Graphical user interface for the desktop

Python has a very clean syntax and short code which makes it ideal for the beginner. Not only that, Python is fun because, rather than spending all your time worrying about the syntax, you get to spend time thinking about what your code is going to do instead.

Python is an old language, developed in the 1980's and being released for the first time in 1991. It was developed because Guido van Rossum wanted to create a language that was easy to understand and that could access the Amoeba system he was working on. That led to Python, an interpreted and extensible language that was named after Monty Python's Flying Circus for no reason other than the creator was a fan!

Python is so much easier to write and to read than many other languages and is one of the most feature-packed. Benefits include:

- **It's free and its open source** – anyone can use Python and anyone can make changes to the source code and distribute it for themselves.

- **Portable** – Python programs can move from one platform to another can be run without the need to make any changes

- **Embeddable and Extensible** – Python code can be combined with bits of another computer language to produce a high-performance code and scripting abilities which are not always available with other languages out of the box

- **Interpreted Language** – Python does a lot of jobs, like garbage collection, memory management and so on automatically. Also, when your code is run, it will automatically be converted into a code that is understood by your computer system

- **Libraries** – Python contains a lot of libraries with much of the code needed to perform common tasks and cut down on the amount of code you need to write

- **Object-Oriented** -   because everything that is in Python is an object, it is far easier to solve complex problems – each can be broken down into smaller problems through the creation of objects

Python is backed up with a large active community who are constantly striving to improve the language for beginners and experts alike. Use this community as they are of invaluable help to you.

If you are quite ready, we are going to look at the basics of Python programming now. First, I will show you how to install it on your computer and then we will go through the basic concepts. There are going to be plenty of examples for you to input into Python and try or yourself. This is the best way to learn so I urge you to get your Python environment set up and work along with this book – you will learn so much more than if you just read it.☐

Thanks to www.programiz.com for some of the code in this book

Chapter 1: Installing Python and Setting up Your Environment

Python is a multi-platform programming language and I am going to show you how to set it up on Mac OS X and on Windows. Please follow these instructions carefully and get yourself comfortable with using Python, ready for the active examples that follow in the next few chapters.

Mac OS X

1. On the internet, find and open the official Python download page

2. Choose the latest version of Python for Mac OS X and wait for it to download

3. Now locate the download, open it and follow the instructions contained in it to install Python. When finished you will see a message that says, "The installation was successful"

4. Next, you will need a text editor – the recommended one is called Sublime Text so download it from the official website following the instructions on the site. You will be downloading an image file

5. Now open Sublime text and click on **File>New File**

6. Now click on **Save** and call your program myfirstprogram.py – remember where you saved it!

7. Now copy the code below into your new program and save it again:

```
print("Hello, World!")
```

This is the program that all beginners start on and the output should simply be

```
Hello, World!
```

8. Now click on **Tool>Build** and the above output should how up at the bottom of the editor.

Windows

1. Go to the official Python download page and download the latest version for your system
2. Double-click the downloaded file to open it and install it following the instructions given in the file
3. The Python installation on Windows also includes IDLE, which is the best graphical user interface to work with
4. Open IDLE and click on **File>New Window**. Click on **Save** and call the file myfirstprogram.py. Remember where the file is saved to for future use!

Now you can type this code in and press on Save again

```
print("Hello, World!")
```

The output will be

```
Hello, World!
```

Now click on **Run>Run Module** and the output will show up.

Your First Python Program

The Hello, World program is the first one that beginners always learn and it is one of the simplest, as you have already seen. So, open a new file and input the following code – we are now going to write a program that adds 2 numbers together:

```
# Add two numbers

num1 = 4

num2 = 6

sum = num1+num2

print(sum)
```

Now let's look at this program line by line:

- Line 1 - #Add two numbers

If a line begins with #, it is a comment. These are used by programmers to describe what is happening in a code and are designed to help you and others understand what the code is trying to do. Python will ignore any comment as it does not see it a part of the code.

- Line 2 - num1 = 4

num1 is a variable and you will learn more about these later. For now, variables are used to store values and, in this one, we have stored 4

- Line 3 – num2 = 6

Same as line 2 except, this time, we have stored 6 as the value

- Line 4 – sum = num1+num2

We are using the + operator, which you will learn about later, to add the variables, num1 and num2 together. The result will be stored in a further variable called sum

- Line 5 – print(sum)

The print() function is used to display the output or the result on your screen. In this case, it will print 10. Try it and see!

Important Things to Remember

These will help you as you work through this book:

- A Python statement is represented with newline (the Enter key). Semicolons at the end of the statements are optional and should be left off where possible
- Unlike other computer languages where curly braces {} are used to represent a block of code, Python uses indentation, as such:

```
im_a_mum:

 im_a_daughter:

   im_a_grand_daughter

 im_another_daughter:

   im_another_grand_daughter
```

Please note that indentation must be consistent throughout the code.

Chapter 2: Python Keywords, Identifiers, and Operators

Keywords

Like all computer programming languages, Python has a set of keywords, words that are reserved for specific use by Python. These words cannot be used when you are naming identifiers, such as functions or variables – they are for defining structure and syntax only.

Python has 33 reserved keywords and case sensitivity must be observed always when using them. All the keywords are in lowercase except for True, False and None. These are the keywords:

- and
- as
- assert
- break
- class
- continue
- def
- del
- elif
- else
- except
- False
- finally
- for
- from
- global
- if
- import
- in
- is
- lambda
- None
- nonlocal
- not
- or
- pass
- raise
- return
- True
- try
- while
- with
- yield

Identifiers

An identifier is a name that Python gives to entities in Python, such as functions, class, variable, etc. These identifiers, or names, help us to tell the difference between them. There are rules that we must abide by when naming our identifiers:

- They must be a combination of lowercase letters (a to z), uppercase letters (A to Z) and/or digits)0 to 9) or an underscore (_). For example, myClass and myClass1 are valid
- The name must not begin with a digit. For example, myClass1 is valid but 1myClass is not
- As mentioned above, you cannot use a keyword as an identifier

Look at this example:

```
>>> global = 1

  File "<interactive input>", line 1

    global = 1

          ^
```

Type this in and the output will be:

```
SyntaxError: invalid syntax
```

This is because we tried to use the keyword, global, as a name

- We also cannot use any special symbols, such as %, #, @ $ or ! in the name.

Take this example:

```
>>> a@ = 0

  File "<interactive input>", line 1
    a@ = 0

     ^
```

The output will be:

```
SyntaxError: invalid syntax
```

Again, this is because we tried to use a special symbol in the name

- Lastly, an identifier name can be any length but try to keep it reasonable and make the name relevant to the identifier.

Things to Watch Out For:

- Be aware of the case sensitivity in Python. Variable and variable will be two different identifiers!
- Keep your names sensible – c = 9 is perfectly valid by count = 9 is even better because you don't have to figure out what it means
- If your identifier name contains several words, you may separate them using the underscore character; for example, this_is_a_long_name
- Camel-case is also acceptable. In this, we capitalize the first letter of every word in the name EXCEPT for the first one, for example, thisIsALongName

Operators

Python operators are symbols used for specific logical or arithmetical computation and the value that they operate or work on is called an operand. Fr example:

```
>>> 3+6

9
```

In this example, the operator is the + symbol and it performs addition. The operands are 3 and 6 and 9 is the output.

Python has several different operators:

- **Arithmetic**

These are used for mathematical operations, such as subtraction, addition, division and multiplication. The operators are:

Operator	Meaning
+	Adds two operands
-	Subtracts the operand on the right from the one on the left
*	Multiplies two operands
/	Divides the operand on the left by the one on the right
%	Modulus – the reminder after the division of the left operand by the right operand

//	Floor division – a division with a result of a whole number that is adjusted left in the number line
**	Exponent – the left operand raised to the power of the right

Examples of the Arithmetic Operators

```
x = 12

y = 5

# Output: x + y = 17

print('x + y =',x+y)

# Output: x - y = 7

print('x - y =',x-y)

# Output: x * y = 60

print('x * y =',x*y)

# Output: x / y = 2.4

print('x / y =',x/y)

# Output: x // y = 2

print('x // y =',x//y)

# Output: x ** y = 248832

print('x ** y =',x**y)
```

Run the program in your interpreter and the output should be:

```
x + y = 17

x - y = 7

x * y = 60

x / y = 2.4

x // y = 2

x ** y = 248832
```

- ## **Comparison**

The comparison is used to compare values and the output will always be True or False, depending on the condition. These are the comparison operators:

Operator	Meaning
>	Greater than. Results in True if the left operand is greater than the right operand
<	Less than. Results in True if the les operand is less than the right operand
==	Equal to. Results in True if both operands are equal
!=	Not Equal to. Results in True if the operands are not equal
>=	Greater than or equal to. Results in True if the operand on the left is greater than or is equal to the one on the right
<=	Less than or equal to. Results in True if the left operand is less than or is equal to the right operand

Examples of the Comparison Operators

```
x = 12

y = 14

# Output: x > y is False

print('x > y  is',x>y)
```

```python
# Output: x < y is True
print('x < y  is',x<y)
# Output: x == y is False
print('x == y is',x==y)
# Output: x != y is True
print('x != y is',x!=y)
# Output: x >= y is False
print('x >= y is',x>=y)
# Output: x <= y is True
print('x <= y is',x<=y)
```

- ## Logical

The logical operators are:

- and – Results in True if both operands are true
- or – Results in True if either of the operands is true
- not – Results in True if the operand is false

Examples of the Logical Operators:

Logical operators are the and, or, not operators.

```python
x = True
y = False
# Output: x and y is False
print('x and y is',x and y)
# Output: x or y is True
print('x or y is',x or y)
# Output: not x is False
print('not x is',not x)
```

- **Assignment**

The assignment operators are used for assigning a value to a variable. For example, a = 5 is a very simple assignment where the value of 5 is assigned to the variable called a.

There are a few compound operators, like a += 5 that will add the variable and then later assign the same. This is the same as a = a + 5. These are the assignment operators:

Operator	Meaning	
=	x = 5	
+=	x += 5	equivalent to x = x + 5
-=	x -= 5	equivalent to x = x – 5
*=	x *= 5	equivalent to x = x * 5
/=	x /= 5	equivalent to x = x / 5
%=	x %= 5	equivalent to x = x % 5
//=	x //= 5	equivalent to x = x // 5
**=	x **= 5	equivalent to x = x ** = 5
&=	x &= 5	equivalent to x = x & 5
|=	x |= 5	equivalent to x = x | 5
^=	x ^= 5	equivalent to x = x ^ 5
>>=	x >> = 5	equivalent to x = x >> 5
<<=	x << = 5	equivalent to x = x << 5

Special Operators

Python also offers a few special operators, such as the membership or the identity operator.

• Identity

The two identity operators are is and is not. We use these to see if two variables or values are on the same piece of memory. Please note; if two variables are equal it doesn't automatically follow that they are identical.

Operator	Meaning
is	Results in True if both operands are referring to the same object, i.e. they are identical
is not	Results in True if both operands are not referring to the same object, i.e. are not identical

Examples of the Identity Operators

```
x1 = 4
y1 = 4
x2 = 'Hi'
y2 = 'Hi'
x3 = [5, 6, 7]
y3 = [5, 6, 7]
# Output: False
print(x1 is not y1)
# Output: True
print(x2 is y2)
# Output: False
print(x3 is y3)
```

In this example, x1 and y1 are both integers and both have the same value. This means they are equal and they are identical. The same is true of the strings x2 and y2. However, x3 and y3 are lists (you will learn about these later in the book) – they are equal but they are not identical. Lists are mutable, which means they can be changed so the interpreter will put them separately in the memory even though they are equal

- **Membership**

The two membership operators are in and not in. These are used for testing whether values or variables are to be found in a sequence, which could be a list, a string, a tuple, a set or a dictionary. Note that, in the dictionary, we cannot test for a value, only for the presence of a key.

Operator	Meaning
in	Results in True if the variable or value specified is in the sequence
not in	Results in True if the variable or value specified is not in the sequence

Examples of the Membership Operators

```
x = 'Hi folks!'
y = {1:'a',2:'b'}
# Output: True
print('H' in x)
# Output: True
print('hi' not in x)
# Output: True
print(1 in y)
# Output: False
print('a' in y)
```

In this example, H can be found in x but hi is not – don't forget the case sensitivity. In the same way, 1 is a key while a is the value found in dictionary y and, as such, a in y will return False.

Chapter 3: Python Flow Control

Otherwise known as decision making, this is needed when we need a piece of code to execute ONLY if a specified condition is met. There are a few statements that we use for this:

If Statement

The syntax for the if statement is:

```
if test expression:

    statement(s)
```

The program will evaluate the test expression and if it evaluates to True, the statement will be executed accordingly. Should the test expression evaluate to False, the statement will be ignored.

Python uses indentation to indicate the if statement body- the indentation marks the start and the statement ends at the first line that is not indented.

All non-zero values are interpreted as True while 0 or None values are False.

Try this example of an if statement:

```
# If the number should be positive, we will print a
relevant message

num = 4

if num > 0:

    print(num, "This is a positive number.")

print("This will be printed.")

num = -2
```

```
if num > 0:

    print(num, "This is a positive number.")

print("This will also be printed.")
```

Run the program and the output should be:

```
4 This is a positive number

This will always be printed

This will also be printed.
```

In this example, the test expression is num > 0 and the if statement body will only be executed if this is True. When the variable called num is equal to 4, the expression evaluates True so the statement body inside the body is executed. When the variable called num is equal to -2, the expression is False and that body is then ignored.

Note that the print() statement is outside of the indented code and is not part of the if code block – this means it will always be executed, no matter what the result of the test expression is.

If...else Statement

The syntax of the if...else statement is

```
if test expression:

    Body of if

else:

    Body of else
```

This statement is used for evaluating a test expression and the body of the if statement will only execute should the condition result in True. If the condition results in False, the body of the else statement will be executed. Again, we use indentation to separate each code block. This is an example of the if...else statement:

```python
# The program will look to see if the number is positive or negative

# And will display a relevant message

num = 5

# Try these as well.

# num = -7

# num = 0

if num >= 0:

    print("Positive or Zero")

else:

    print("Negative number")
```

In this example, when num is equal to 5, the test expression will be True and the if body will be executed; in this case, the else body is ignored. However, if num were equal to -7, the test expression would be False; in this case, the if body is ignored and the else body is executed. If num equals 0 then it is True and the if body will be executed, ignoring the else body

If...elif...else

The syntax of the if...elif...else statement is:

```python
if test expression:

    Body of if

elif test expression:

    Body of elif
```

```
else:

    Body of else
```

Elif is a shortened version of else...if and we use it when we want to check several expressions. If the test expression for the if body is False, the condition in the subsequent elif body will be checked and this will continue until one evaluates to True, in which case, the statement will be executed, or all expressions evaluate to False, in which case the else body would be executed.

Note that only ONE of the blocks in the elif statements can be executed as per the condition – as soon as one evaluates to True, the rest will be ignored.

An if block may only have one else block but it can contain several elif blocks. Have a look at this example:

```python
# In the program,

# we can check whether the number is positive or

# negative or zero and

# display the right message

num = 3.2

# Try these as well:

# num = 0

# num = -4.4

if num > 0:

    print("Positive number")

elif num == 0:

    print("Zero")

else:
```

```
print("Negative number")
```

When the variable called num is a positive number, then the output will be

```
Positive number
```

If num is equal to 0 then the output will be

```
Zero
```

And if num is a negative number then the output will be

```
Negative Number
```

Nested if statements

Now we start to go a bit deeper. It is perfectly possible to place an if...elif...else statement inside another one and we call this 'nesting'. There is no limit to the number of statements that you can nest so indentation is very important to sort out how deep the nesting goes. In all truthfulness, it can get incredibly confusing so, where you can, please avoid using this.

Try this example and you will see just how confusing it can get!

```
# In the program, we will input a number

# check to see if the number is positive or

# negative or zero and display

# the right message

# This time we use the nested if

num = float(input("Enter a number: "))

if num >= 0:

    if num == 0:
```

```
        print("Zero")
    else:
        print("Positive number")
else:
    print("Negative number")
```

Output 1

Enter a number: 4

Positive number

Output 2

Enter a number: -1

Negative number

Output 3

Enter a number: 0

Zero

For Loops

for loops are used for when you want to iterate over a sequence, be it a tuple, a list or a string, for example. We call this 'traversal'. The syntax of the for loop is:

```
for val in sequence:

    Body of for
```

val is a variable and it will take the value of the item in your sequence on every iteration. The loop will continue until it gets to the last item. We separate the for loop body from the code by using indentation.

This is an example of the for loop:

```
# A program that finds the sum of all the numbers
stored in a list

# List of numbers

numbers = [4, 2, 1, 9, 5, 6, 7, 1, 13]

# variable to store the sum

sum = 0

# iterate over the list

for val in numbers:

    sum = sum+val

# Output: The sum is 48

print("The sum is", sum)
```

Run this and you should see the following as the output:

```
The sum is 48
```

The range() function

The range() function is used as a way of generating a sequence of numbers. For example, range(9) would generate a sequence of 9 numbers, from 0 to 8. Important – Python indexing begins at 0 so, where you would expect range(9) to end at 9, it counts 0 as the first number, thus ending at 8.

We are also able to define the stop, start and step size in the range() function, as such:

- range(start)
- range(stop)
- range(step size)

If you do not provide a step size, it will default to 1.

The range90 function will not store every value in memory because it would just be too inefficient. So, it will remember the start and the stop and it will remember the step size and the next number in the range is generated on the go. If we wanted to force range() to output all the items in the sequence we would use another function, called list().

Try this example:

```
# Output: range(0, 10)

print(range(10))

# Output: [0, 1, 2, 3, 4, 5, 6, 7, 8, 9]

print(list(range(10)))

# Output: [2, 3, 4, 5, 6, 7]

print(list(range(2, 8)))

# Output: [2, 5, 8, 11, 14, 17]

print(list(range(2, 20, 3)))
```

The range() function can be used in a for loop as a way of iterating through a number sequence and we can also combine it with a function called len() to use indexing for iterating through the sequence. Have a look at this example:

```
# A program that iterates through a list using indexing

genre = [metal, blues, rock]

# iterate over the list using index

for i in range(len(genre)):

    print("I like", genre[i])
```

When you run the program, the output will be:

```
I like metal

I like blues

I like rock
```

For loop with else

The for loop may also have an else block if needed. The else block will only be executed if the sequence items in the for loop run out. To stop the for loop, we use a break statement and then the else part of the statement will be ignored.

Have a look at this example:

```python
digits = [0, 2, 6]

for i in digits:

    print(i)

else:

    print("No items left.")
```

If you run this the output should be

```
0

2

6

No items left.
```

The for loop is going to print the list items until the loop finishes, at which point the loop will execute the else body, printing:

```
No items left.
```

While Loop

while loops are used for iteration over code blocks for as long as text expression evaluates True. This is normally used when we don't know how many times we need to iterate. The syntax of a while loop is:

```
while test_expression:

    Body of while
```

In this loop, the test expression will be checked first and the loop body will only be gone into if test_expression is True. After one sequence iteration, the test expression will be checked again. If it still evaluates to True, the iteration will continue. Only when that test expression evaluates to False will the iteration stop.

As with all statements, indentation is used to determine the start of the while loop and it ends at the first line that is not indented.

Have a look at this example:

```python
# A program to add natural

# numbers up to

# sum = 1+2+3+...+n

# To take an input from the user,

# n = int(input("Enter n: "))

n = 10

# initialize sum and counter

sum = 0
```

```
i = 1

while i <= n:

    sum = sum + i

    i = i+1    # update counter

# print the sum

print("The sum is", sum)
```

Run this program and you should get an output of:

```
Enter n: 10

The sum is 55
```

In this example, the test expression will evaluate True for as long as the counter variable called i is equal to or less than 10.

The counter variable value must be increased inside the loop body – do not forget to do this as you will end up with an infinite loop, one that never stops!

While loop with else

In the same way as the for loop, the while loop may also have an else block if needed. The else block will only be executed should the test expression in the while loop evaluates False. Again, we can use a break statement to terminate the while loop. In this case, the else block will be ignored.

Have a look at this example:

```
# This example illustrates

# the use of else statement

# with the while loop

counter = 0
```

```
while counter < 3:

    print("Inside loop")

    counter = counter + 1

else:

    print("Inside else")
```

The output of this will be:

```
Inside loop

Inside loop

Inside loop

Inside else
```

The counter variable is used to print the string that says, 'Inside loop' three times over. On the fourth time, the test condition evaluates False and the else body is then executed

Break and continue statements are used to change the way a normal loop flows. On occasion, you will want the iteration to stop or you may want to terminate the entire loop without first checking the test expressions and these two statements come in very handy.

Break Statement

The break statement is used to terminate the loop the statement is in and control will go straight to the statement that immediately follows the loop body. If the break statement is used in a nested loop, it will terminate the inner loop. This is the syntax used:

```
break
```

And this is an example of the break statement in use:

```
# Using the break statement inside loop

for val in "string":

    if val == "i":

        break

    print(val)

print("The end")
```

The output will be:

```
s

t

r

The end
```

We iterated through the sequence 'string' and we checked to see if the letter 'i' is there, at which point we break out of the loop. As you can see from the output, all the letters in the sequence up to 'i' are printed.

Continue Statement

We use the continue statement to ignore the remaining code in a loop ONLY for the current iteration. The loop does not terminate; instead, it carries on with the next iteration. The syntax of the continue statement is:

```
continue
```

And this is an example of the continue statement in use

```
# This program uses the continue statement inside loops

for val in "string":

    if val == "i":

        continue

    print(val)

print("The end")
```

The output will be:

```
s

t

r

n

g

The end
```

This is the same example as the break statement except we used the continue statement instead. Provided the string is not 'i' the loop continues and does not execute the remainder of the block. As you can see from the output, all the letters in the string are printed except for 'i'.

Chapter 4: Python Functions

A Python function is a group of statements, each related, that perform a certain task. Functions are useful for breaking our code down into smaller and more manageable chunks; as your program grows in size, the use of functions can make it more manageable and better organized as well as helping you to avoid repeating yourself and enables your code to be reused elsewhere.

The syntax of a function is:

```
def function_name(parameters):

    """docstring"""

    statement(s)
```

This function has the following in it:

- The def keyword begins the function header
- A name is given to the function to identify it
- Parameters are provided – these are the arguments that the values are passed through to the function and are optional
- A colon is used to define the end of the function header
- A docstring is used to describe what the function is for – this is optional
- At least one valid statement for the body of the function – remember the indentation
- A return statement for returning a value from your function- this is optional

This is an example of a function:

```
def greet(name):

    """This function will greet

    the person who is passed in as

    parameter"""

    print("Hi, " + name + ". Good Morning!")
```

Function Calls

Once the function has been defined, it may then be called from another function, another program or from the Python prompt. T do this, we type the name of the function and the parameters we want to use:

```
>>> greet('Aaron')

Hi, Aaron. Good Morning!
```

Docstring

After the function header, you may input a string which is known as the docstring This is optional but useful because it describes what the function does.

In the example above, we used a docstring straight after the header. These are enclosed in triple quotes ("" or """") so that we can take the docstring over several lines if needed. To call this, we use the _doc_ attribute. For example:

```
>>> print(greet.__doc__)

This function will greet

    the person who is passed into the

    name parameter
```

Return Statement

We use a return statement when we want to come out of a function and return to the point at which the function was called. The syntax of return is:

return [expression_list]

The return statement may include an expression which will be evaluated with the value being returned. If no expression is put in the statement or the return statement is not included, the return will be the object called None. Have a go at this example:

```
>>> print(greet("Linda"))

Hello, Linda. Good Morning!

None
```

The output is the returned value of None

Have a go at this example of a return statement:

```
def absolute_value(num):

    """This function will return the absolute

    value of the entered number"""

    if num >= 0:

        return num

    else:

        return -num

# Output: 2

print(absolute_value(2))

# Output: 4

print(absolute_value(-4))
```

Scope and Lifetime of a Variable

Variable scope refers to the part of a computer code where that variable is recognized. A variable and its parameters that are defined within a function cannot be seen from outside that function so they are given a 'local' scope.

The lifetime of the variable refers to the time in which the variable remains in memory and this will be for as long as that function executes. Once we return from a function, that function is then destroyed and will not remember any variable values from previous calls.

This example shows you the variable scope in a function:

```python
def my_func():

    x = 10

    print("Value inside function:",x)

x = 20

my_func()

print("Value outside function:",x)
```

The output will be:

```
Value inside function: 10

Value outside function: 20
```

To start with, x has a value of 20. Despite the fact that my_func() changed that value to 10, the value that was outside the function was not affected. The reason for this is that the variable x that is inside the function is local to that function. The variables that are outside the function are called 'global' variables because they can be seen from inside the function.

Both variables have the same name but they have different scope and, as such, are not the same variable.

Global scope variables can only be read from inside a function; they cannot be changed. If you wanted to modify a variable value that is outside of a function, you would need to specify that by using the global keyword to declare them as global variables.

Function Types:

Functions can be divided into two types:

- Built-in
- User-defined

The built-in functions are self-explanatory – they are already written and available in Python.

User-defined functions are those that we define to do something specific the advantages of using these are that they can help us chop a large program into smaller chunks, making your code easier to read and understand, easier to maintain and a whole lot easier to debug. If you need to repeat code throughout your program, you can define functions to use that code and then call the function to execute it rather than continually typing the same thing repeatedly.

An example of a user-defined function is:

```python
# This program will illustrate

# how to use a user-defined functions

def add_numbers(x,y):

    sum = x + y

    return sum
```

```
num1 = 5

num2 = 6

print("The sum is", add_numbers(num1, num2))
```

The output will be:

```
Enter a number: 2.4

Enter another number: 6.5

The sum is 8.9
```

The function called my_addition is user-defined and it adds a pair of numbers, returning the result. We could have done the multiplication in the function if we wanted but defining your own function makes it easier.

Note – there are three built-in functions in the above example:

- input()
- print()
- float()

Function Arguments

Functions may be defined to take a variable number of different arguments. Have a look at this example of a function called with arguments:

```
def greet(name,msg):

    """This function will greet

    the person who has the message"""

    print("Hello",name + ', ' + msg)

greet("Simeon","Good Morning!")
```

The output will be:

```
Hello Simeon, Good Morning!
```

In this example, there are two parameters with the function called greet(). Because of this, the function runs very smoothly and there are no errors. If we were to call that function with another number of arguments, the interpreter would not be happy. The next example shows you the call to the function with one argument and with no arguments, together with the error messages you would see:

```
>>> greet("Simeon")    # just one argument

TypeError:   greet()   missing  1  required  positional
argument: 'msg'

>>> greet()    # no arguments

TypeError:   greet()   missing  2  required  positional
arguments: 'name' and 'msg'
```

Variable Function Arguments

Until this point, we used functions with a fixed number of arguments but we can define functions to take a variable number. There are three forms of this:

- ### Default Arguments

Function arguments may have a default value and we can provide this through the assignment operator (=). Look at this example:

```
def greet(name, msg = "Good Morning!"):

    """

    This function will greet

    the person who has the
```

```
    provided message.

    If message has not been provided,

    it will default to "Good

    Morning!"

    """

    print("Hello",name + ', ' + msg)
greet("Paula")

greet("Barry","How do you do?")
```

The name of the parameter has not been given a default value and is a requirement during a call. However, the parameter called msg does have a default value, which is 'Good Morning!' and, as such, is optional during the call. Should a value be provided, the default value will be overwritten.

Any of the arguments in a function can be given default values but as soon as there is a default argument, every argument to the right of it should also be given default values. What this means is that an argument with no default value may not follow any argument that does have a default value. The following example shows   the function header from above defined as:

```
def greet(msg = "Good Morning!", name):
```

This would result in an error:

```
SyntaxError:   non-default   argument   follows   default
argument
```

Keyword Arguments

When a function is called with values, those values are assigned by position to the arguments. For example, in the greet() function above, when we called greet(:Barry", "How do you do?") "Barry" is assigned to the name of the argument while the greeting gets assigned to msg.

Python lets you call a function using keyword arguments and by doing this, the order of the arguments may be changed. All the calls in the following example are valid and they all have the same result:

```
>>> # 2 keyword arguments

>>> greet(name = "Barry",msg = "How do you do?")



>>> # 2 keyword arguments (out of order)

>>> greet(msg = "How do you do?",name = "Barry")



>>> # 1 positional, 1 keyword argument

>>> greet("Barry",msg = "How do you do?")
```

As you can see, positional arguments and keyword arguments may be combined when we call a function but you do need to bear in mind that the keyword arguments come after the positional arguments, not before. If you put the keyword argument first, you will get errors, as in this example:

```
greet(name="Barry","How do you do?")
```

```
The error would be:
```

```
SyntaxError: non-keyword arg after keyword arg
```

Arbitrary Arguments

You won't always know how many arguments are to be passed to a function so Python lets you use arbitrary arguments. The * is used in the function definition, in front of the parameter name, as a notation that you are using arbitrary arguments. Have a look at his example:

```python
def greet(*names):

    """This function will greet all

    of the people in the names tuple."""

    # names is a tuple with arguments

    for name in names:

        print("Hello",name)

greet("Mary","Mark","Simon","Harry")
```

The output will be:

```
Hello Mary

Hello Mark

Hello Simon

Hello Harry
```

The function has been called with several arguments, all of which are put into a tuple (more about these later) and then passed to the function. In the function, the for loop is used to get all those arguments back.

Chapter 5: Python Datatypes

Python supports three main datatypes – the integer, the floating-point number and complex numbers. These are defined, respectively, as int, float, and complex. The int and float are different in that int is a whole number while float has a decimal point. For example, 4 is an int while is a float. The complex number is written as x + yj. X is the real part of the equation while yj is an imaginary part.

To determine the class that a variable or a value belongs to, we can use the type() function. For example:

```
# Output: <class 'int'>

print(type(a))

# Output: <class 'float'>

print(type(4.0))

# Output: (7+3j)

c = 4 + 3j

print(c + 3)

# Output: True

print(isinstance(c, complex))
```

An integer may be any length but the floating-point numbers will only be accurate to 15 decimal places – anything longer than that and it becomes inaccurate. The numbers that we deal with on a daily basis are decimal but computer programmers work in binary, octal and hexadecimal systems. To represent these numbers in Python, we use a prefix in front of the number:

System	Prefix
Binary	ob or OB
Octal	Oo or oO
Hexadecimal	Ox or oX

Have a look at these examples:

```
# Output: 107

print(0b1101011)

# Output: 253 (251 + 2)

print(0xFB + 0b10)

# Output: 13

print(0o15)
```

Run this program, the output should be:

```
107

253

13
```

Type Conversion

Python allows us to convert one number type to another, often called coercion. If one of the operands is a float, operations such as subtraction or addition will implicitly coerce the integer to a float. For example:

```
>>> 2 + 3.0

5.0
```

As you can see, the integer, 2, has been coerced to a float, 2.0 for the addition and the result is also a float.

Built-in functions, like float(), int() and complex() can be used to convert implicitly between types, even converting from strings. For example:

```
>>> int(2.2)

2

>>> int(-2.6)

-2

>>> float(7)

7.0

>>> complex(2+4j')

(2+4j)
```

When you convert from a float to an int, the number becomes truncated, i.e. it becomes an int that is closer to Zero.

Decimal

The built-in float() class will also perform a few calculations that are surprising. Let's say that we add 1.2 to 2.1 – we know that the result is 3.3 but Python won't agree with you. Type the following into your interpreter and see what happens:

```
>>> (1.2 + 2.1) == 3.3

False
```

Why did we get that result?

Floating-point numbers are implemented as binary fractions because your computer can only understand binary numbers. Because of this, pretty much all the decimal fractions will not be accurately stored on your computer.

Let's take the following example. The fraction, 1/3, cannot be represented in decimal because the result would be 0.3333333333 recurring – this is too long and we are only able to approximate it. The decimal fraction, 0.1, results in a long binary fraction that is infinite – 0.00011001100110011... and so on. The computer is only able to store a finite number not an infinite number. So, this approximates 0.1 but it can never be equal so the error does not lie with Python; it is in the limitations of the hardware we use.

```
>>> 1.2 + 2.1

3.3000000000000003
```

To get over this, Python includes a decimal module. Users can set the precision manually, overriding the 15-place precision for decimal numbers.

```
import decimal

# Output: 0.1

print(0.1)

#                                              Output:
Decimal('0.1000000000000000055511151231257827021181583404541015625')

print(decimal.Decimal(0.1))
```

We use this module for decimal calculations similar to those that you learned (or not) in school and it will also retain significance. We know that the weight 27.50 kg is far more accurate than 27.5 kg because there are two decimal places and not one.

```
from decimal import Decimal as D

# Output: Decimal('3.3')

print(D('1.2') + D('2.1'))

# Output: Decimal('3.000')

print(D('1.2') * D('2.50'))
```

The only reason we do not use the decimal module instead of float at all times is that it isn't efficient to do so. Float operations are significantly faster than decimal operations.

Decimal should be used in these cases:

- when you use financial applications that require an exact decimalization
- when you need control over the precision level
- when you carry out operations similar to the ones you did at school

Fractions

The fractions module is used for fractional number operations. Fractions have both a numerator and a denominator and both of these are integers. The faction module supports rational number arithmetic. Fraction objects may be created in several ways:

```
import fractions

# Output: 3/2

print(fractions.Fraction(1.5))

# Output: 5

print(fractions.Fraction(5))

# Output: 1/3

print(fractions.Fraction(1,3))
```

When you create a fraction from a float, you might see some strange results. The reason for this is because of the 15-place decimal accuracy that we talked about earlier. Thankfully, the preferred method of instantiating with strings is allowed with the Fraction module:

```python
import fractions

# As float

# Output: 2476979795053773/2251799813685248

print(fractions.Fraction(1.1))

# As string

# Output: 11/10

print(fractions.Fraction('1.1'))
```

This datatype provides support for all the basic operations, like this:

```python
from fractions import Fraction as F

# Output: 2/3

print(F(1,3) + F(1,3))

# Output: 6/5

print(1 / F(5,6))

# Output: False

print(F(-3,10) > 0)

# Output: True

print(F(-3,10) < 0)
```

Chapter 6: Python Lists

Python contains several compound datatypes which are sometimes called sequences. The most common is the List, an incredibly versatile datatype.

How to create a list?

Lists are created by putting all the elements or items inside a set of square brackets [], with each item separated from the next by a comma. A list can have as many elements as you need it to and you can use a mixture of different datatypes, like int, string, float, etc.

```
# empty list

my_list = []
```

```
# list of integers

my_list = [4, 5, 6]
```

```
# list that has mixed datatypes

my_list = [2, "Hello", 3.5]
```

A list may also contain another list as one of the items and these are known as nested lists:

```
# nested list

my_list = ["mouse", [8, 4, 6], ['a']]
```

How to access elements from a list?

List elements can be accessed in several ways:

- ### **List Index**

The index operator [] can be used to access items in a list. Don't forget the index begins at 0 so a list of 5 elements will run from index 0 to index 4. Attempting to access any element other than this will result in an IndexError. The index cannot be anything other than an integer otherwise a TypeError will be raised.

To access a nested list, we use nested indexing:

```
my_list = ['g','r','a','v','e']

# Output: g

print(my_list[0])

# Output: a

print(my_list[2])

# Output: e

print(my_list[4])

# Error! Only an integer can be used for indexing

# my_list[4.0]

# Nested List

n_list = ["Happy", [2,0,1,7]]

# Nested indexing

# Output: a

print(n_list[0][1])

# Output: 5
```

```python
print(n_list[1][3])
```

• **Negative indexing**

Negative indexing is also allowed for sequences and an index of -1 will refer to the last item in the sequence, -2 is the second to last and so on:

```python
my_list = ['g','r','a','v','e']

# Output: e

print(my_list[-1])

# Output: g

print(my_list[-5])
```

• **Slicing Lists**

A range of items in one list can be accessed with the slicing operator, which is a colon:

```python
my_list = ['e','m','b','e','z','z','l','e','r']

# elements 3rd to 5th

print(my_list[2:5])

# elements beginning to 4th

print(my_list[:-5])

# elements 6th to end

print(my_list[5:])

# elements beginning to end

print(my_list[:])
```

Changing or Adding Elements

A list is mutable and this means that, unlike the string and the tuple, which we will discuss in the next chapters, the elements may be changed. To change one item or a range of items, we use the assignment operator (=):

```python
# mistake values

odd = [4, 6, 8, 10]

# change the 1st item

odd[0] = 1

# Output: [2, 6, 8, 10]

print(odd)

# change 2nd to 4th items

odd[1:4] = [5, 7, 9]

# Output: [2, 5, 7, 9]

print(odd)
```

We can use the append() method to add an item to a list or, if we wanted to add several items, we would use the extend() method:

```python
odd = [3, 5, 7]

odd.append(9)

# Output: [3, 5, 7, 9]

print(odd)

odd.extend([11, 13, 15])

# Output: [3, 5, 7, 9, 11, 13, 15]

print(odd)
```

The addition operator (+) can also be used to combine lists together, otherwise known as concatenation while the * operator will repeat the list for a specified number of times:

```
odd = [1, 3, 5]
```

```
# Output: [1, 3, 5, 9, 7, 5]

print(odd + [9, 7, 5])
```

```
#Output: ["re", "re", "re"]

print(["re"] * 3)
```

We may also add an item at a specified location using the insert() method or we can add several items by squeezing them into an empty slice in a list

```
odd = [1, 9]

odd.insert(1,3)

# Output: [1, 3, 9]

print(odd)

odd[2:2] = [5, 7]

# Output: [1, 3, 5, 7, 9]

print(odd)
```

Deleting or Removing List Elements

Elements can be deleted from a list with the del keyword; we can even use it to delete an entire list

```
my_list = ['a','c','a','d','e','m','y']
```

```python
# delete one item
del my_list[2]
# Output: ['a', 'c', 'd', 'e', 'm', 'y']
print(my_list)
# delete multiple items
del my_list[1:5]
# Output: ['a', 'y']
print(my_list)
# delete entire list
del my_list
# Error: List not defined
print(my_list)
```

The remove() method may be used to remove a specified item or we can use pop() to remove an item at a specified index. The pop()method is used to remove the last item and return it if an index is not given. This helps in the implementation of lists as stacks, i.e. a data structure of first in, last out.

We can also empty a list by using the clear() method:

```python
my_list = ['a','c','a','d','e','m','y']
my_list.remove('a')
# Output: ['c', 'a', 'd', 'e', 'm', 'y']
print(my_list)
# Output: 'a'
print(my_list.pop(1))
```

```
# Output: ['c', 'd', 'e', 'm', 'y']

print(my_list)

# Output: 'y'

print(my_list.pop())

# Output: ['c', 'd', 'e', 'm']

print(my_list)

my_list.clear()

# Output: []

print(my_list)
```

Lastly, we can assign a slice of elements with an empty list to delete the list items:

```
>>> my_list = ['a','c','a','d','e','m','y']

>>> my_list[2:3] = []

>>> my_list

['a', 'c', 'd', 'e', 'm', 'y']

>>> my_list[2:5] = []

>>> my_list

['a', 'c', 'y']
```

List Methods

Lists have some methods available to them and they are accessed by using list.method(). These are the methods available to list:

Method	Function
append()	adds an element at the end of a list
extend()	adds the elements in one list to another list
insert()	inserts an item at the specified index
remove()	removes a specified item from the list
pop()	removes an item and returns it at the specified index
clear()	removes every item from the list
index()	returns the index of the first specified matched item
count()	returns the count of the number of items passed as arguments
sort()	sorts the items in an ascending list
reverse()	reverses the item order in the list
copy()	returns a copy of the list

These are examples of list methods:

```python
my_list = [3, 8, 1, 6, 0, 8, 4]

# Output: 1

print(my_list.index(8))

# Output: 2

print(my_list.count(8))

my_list.sort()
```

```
# Output: [0, 1, 3, 4, 6, 8, 8]

print(my_list)

my_list.reverse()

# Output: [8, 8, 6, 4, 3, 1, 0]

print(my_list)
```

List Comprehension

List comprehension is a nice way to use an existing list to create a new list. An expression is used with a for statement that is included inside a set of square brackets. Have a look at this example of creating a list with each of the items increased by the power of 2:

```
pow2 = [2 ** x for x in range(10)]

# Output: [1, 2, 4, 8, 16, 32, 64, 128, 256, 512]

print(pow2)
```

the equivalent code to this would be:

```
pow2 = []

for x in range(10):

    pow2.append(2 ** x)
```

List comprehension can contain several for statements or if statements if needed. An if statement can be used to filter items out for a new list. Have a look at these examples:

```
>>> pow2 = [2 ** x for x in range(10) if x > 5]

>>> pow2

[64, 128, 256, 512]

>>> odd = [x for x in range(20) if x % 2 == 1]
```

```
>>> odd

[1, 3, 5, 7, 9, 11, 13, 15, 17, 19]

>>> [x+y for x in ['Python ','C '] for y in
['Language','Programming']]

['Python Language', 'Python Programming', 'C Language',
'C Programming']
```

Other List Operations in Python

• List Membership Test

We can test to see if an item is in a specified list by using the in keyword:

```
my_list = ['a','c','a','d','e','m','y']

# Output: True

print('a' in my_list)

# Output: False

print('v' in my_list)

# Output: True

print('b' not in my_list)
```

Iterating Through a List

We can iterate through the items in a list using a for loop:

```
for fruit in ['pineapple','peach','pear']:

    print("I like",fruit)
```

Built-in Functions with List

There are a number of built-in functions that list can use for different things:

Function	Meaning
all()	will return True if all list items are true or if it is an empty list
any()	will return True if any item is true. An empty list will return False
enumerate()	Returns an enumerate object which contains a tuple with the index and value of all the list items
len()	will return the length of the list – the number of items in it
list()	will convert an iterable into a list
max()	will return the biggest item from the list
min()	will return the smallest item form the list
sorted()	will return a new list that has been sorted – it will NOT sort the original list
sum()	Will return the sum of all the list items

Chapter 7: Python Tuples

Tuples are very much like lists with one exception, whereas you can change items in a list when it has been assigned, you cannot change the items in a tuple. The advantages of using the tuple over the list are:

- Tuples are used for different or heterogeneous datatypes while lists are used for similar or homogeneous datatypes
- Tuples are immutable so it is much faster to iterate through than a list is
- Tuples with immutable items can be used as keys for dictionaries
- Tuples are better for data that shouldn't or doesn't change and will ensure that the data is write-protected

Creating a Tuple

To create a tuple, we place all the elements inside a set of parentheses (), although this is optional, and each element is separated by a comma. You can put any number of items in a tuple and they don't have to be the same datatype either.

```
# nested tuple

# Output: ("mouse", [8, 4, 6], (1, 2, 3))

my_tuple = ("mouse", [8, 4, 6], (1, 2, 3))

print(my_tuple)

# You don't need to use parentheses to create a tuple

# also known as tuple packing
```

```
# Output: 3, 4.6, "cat"

my_tuple = 3, 4.6, "cat"

print(my_tuple)

# we can also unpack tuples

# Output:

# 3

# 4.6

# cat

a, b, c = my_tuple

print(a)

print(b)

print(c)
```

It is not easy to create a tuple with a single element. If you have one element inside a set of parentheses, you will need to use a trailing comma to indicate that it is a tuple.

```
# using just parentheses isn't enough

# Output: <class 'str'>

my_tuple = ("hello")

print(type(my_tuple))

# you must add a trailing comma at the end

# Output: <class 'tuple'>

my_tuple = ("hello",)

print(type(my_tuple))

# parentheses are optional
```

```
# Output: <class 'tuple'>

my_tuple = "hello",

print(type(my_tuple))
```

Accessing the Elements in a Tuple

We can access the items in a tuple in several ways:

1. Indexing

The index operator [] can be used to access one item in the tuple where the index begins at 0: So, if a tuple contains 6 elements, the index will run from 0 to 5 – if you tried to access an element after 5, you would get an Index Error. The index has to be an integer so if you tried to use other datatypes, you would get a TypeError.

In the same way, we use nested indexing to access nested tuples, as shown in this example:

```
# the index has to be in range

# If you uncommented line 14,

# you would get an error.

# IndexError: list index out of range

#print(my_tuple[6])

# index has to be an integer

# If you uncommented line 21,

# you would get an error.

# TypeError: list indices have to be integers, not float

#my_tuple[2.0]
```

```python
# nested tuple

n_tuple = ("mouse", [8, 4, 6], (1, 2, 3))

# nested index

# Output: 's'

print(n_tuple[0][3])
```

Running the program would give this output:

```
p

t

s

4
```

2. Negative Indexing

Negative indexing can be used for sequences; -1 refers to the final item, -2 to the second form last, and so on

```python
my_tuple = ('a','l','l','o','w','s')

# Output: 's'

print(my_tuple[-1])

# Output: 'a'

print(my_tuple[-6])
```

3. Slicing

The slicing operator, which is the colon, can also be used to access a range of elements or items

```python
my_tuple = ('e','m','b','e','z','z','l','e','r')

# elements 2nd to 4th
```

```python
# Output: ('m', 'b', 'e')

print(my_tuple[1:4])

# elements beginning to 2nd

# Output: ('e', 'm')

print(my_tuple[:-7])

# elements 8th to end

# Output: ('e', 'r')

print(my_tuple[7:])

# elements beginning to end

# Output: ('e', 'm', 'b', 'e', 'z', 'z', 'l', 'e', 'r')

print(my_tuple[:])
```

Changing a Tuple

Tuples are immutable, which means that the elements may not be changed once the tuple has been assigned. However, if the element in the tuple is mutable, such as a list, the nested items in that item can be changed. Tuples may also be assigned to different values and we call this reassignment

```python
my_tuple = (4, 2, 3, [6, 5])

# we may not change an element

# If you uncommented line 8

# you would get an error:

#  TypeError:  'tuple'  object  doesn't  support  item
assignment

#my_tuple[1] = 9

# but an item that is mutable can be changed
```

```
# Output: (4, 2, 3, [9, 5])

my_tuple[3][0] = 9

print(my_tuple)

# tuples may be reassigned

# Output: ('e', 'm', 'b', 'e', 'z', 'z', 'l', 'e', 'r')

my_tuple = ('e','m','b','e','z','z','l','e','r')

print(my_tuple)
```

The + operator may be used to add two tuples together and this is known as concatenation. The * operator is used to repeat the tuple items for a specified number of times. Both operations will result in the creation of a new tuple

```
# Concatenation

# Output: (4, 5, 6, 7, 8, 9)

print((4, 5, 6) + (7, 8, 9))

# Repeat

# Output: ('Repeat', 'Repeat', 'Repeat')

print(("Repeat",) * 3)
```

Deleting a Tuple

As you know, you cannot change any of the items in a tuple and that means not being able to remove or delete any particular item. However, the entire tuple can be deleted with the del keyword.

```
my_tuple = ('e','m','b','e','z','z','l','e','r')

# cannot delete items
```

```python
# if you uncommented line 8,

# you would get an error:

#  TypeError:  'tuple'  object  doesn't  support  item
deletion

#del my_tuple[3]

# can delete the whole tuple

# NameError: name 'my_tuple' is not defined

del my_tuple

my_tuple
```

Tuple Methods

The tuple does not have any methods that will add or remove an item. In fact, there are only two methods available to tuple:

Method	Description
count(x)	will return the number of items that are equal to x
index(x)	will return the index of the first item equal to x

These are a few examples of tuple methods:

```python
my_tuple = ('p','e','a','c','h',)

# Count

# Output: 2

print(my_tuple.count('e'))

# Index

# Output: 3
```

```
print(my_tuple.index('c'))
```

Other Tuple Operations

1. Tuple Membership Test

We can use the in keyword to see if an item is in a tuple or not

```
my_tuple = ('p','e','a','c','h',)

# In operation

# Output: True

print('p' in my_tuple)

# Output: False

print('b' in my_tuple)

# Not in operation

# Output: True

print('z' not in my_tuple)
```

2. Iterating Through a Tuple

It is possible to iterate through the items in a tuple using a for loop

```
# Output:

# Hello James

# Hello Carrie

for name in ('James','Carrie'):

    print("Hello",name)
```

Built-in Functions with Tuple

There are several built-in functions that will work to do different things with tuples

Function	Description
all()	Will return True if all tuple items are true or if it is an empty tuple
any()	Will return True if any of the items is True and will return False if it is an empty tuple
enumerate()	Will return an enumerate object, containing pairs of index and value from the tuple items
len()	will return the length of the tuple
max()	will return the biggest element
min()	will return the smallest element
sorted()	Will return a new tuple of sorted items – it will not sort the items in the existing tuple
sum()	will return the sum of all the tuple items
tuple()	Will convert a list, dictionary, string or set to a tuple

Chapter 8: Python Strings

Strings are sequences of characters and a character is nothing more than a symbol. Your computer will not deal with a character; instead, it deals with binary numbers which are manipulated into the characters you see on your screen. Python strings are made up of Unicode characters.

How to create a string

To create a string, we enclose the characters within a set of single or double quotes. You may even use triple quotes if you like but we usually leave these for representing multi-line strings or docstrings.

Have a look at this example:

```python
# all of the following strings are the same

my_string = 'Hello'

print(my_string)

my_string = "Hello"

print(my_string)

my_string = '''Hello'''

print(my_string)

# triple quotes around the string can extend

it over multiple lines

my_string = """Hello, welcome to

        the world of Python"""

print(my_string)
```

Run this program from your interpreter; the result should be:

```
Hello

Hello

Hello

Hello, welcome to

        the world of Python
```

How to access characters in a string

To access individual characters within a string, we can use indexing and, to access a range of characters, we can use slicing. Indexing begins at 0 and if you attempt to access a character that is outside of the index range, you will get an Index Error. Like tuples and lists, the index should be an integer and using any other data type will result in a Type Error.

Python also allows for negative indexing; an index of -1 refers to the last them in the string, while -2 refers to the second from last and so on. A range of elements can be accessed with the slicing operator, which is a colon.

```
str = 'embezzler'
print('str = ', str)
#first character
print('str[0] = ', str[0])
#last character
print('str[-1] = ', str[-1])
#slicing 2nd to 5th character
print('str[1:5] = ', str[1:5])
#slicing 6th to 2nd last character
print('str[5:-2] = ', str[5:-2])
```

If you attempted to access any character that was outside of the index, or if you tried to use a decimal number, you would get an error:

```
# index must be in range

>>> my_string[15]

...

IndexError: string index out of range


# index must be an integer

>>> my_string[1.5]

...

TypeError: string indices must be integers
```

If you are trying to access a range, you must have the index that is going to slice the range from the string.

How to change or delete a string

A string is immutable and, as you already know, this means that none of the elements can be changed once the string has been assigned. Instead, we can assign a different string to the same name:

```
>>> my_string = 'embezzler'

>>> my_string[5] = 'a'

...

TypeError:   'str'   object   does   not   support   item
assignment

>>> my_string = "Adder"

>>> my_string

'Adder'
```

Characters can neither be removed nor deleted from a string but we can delete the string altogether by using the del keyword.

```
>>> del my_string[1]

...

TypeError: 'str' object doesn't support item deletion

>>> del my_string

>>> my_string

...

NameError: name 'my_string' is not defined
```

String Operations

Lots of different operations can be carried out with a string and this is why it is one of the most versatile and commonly used of all the datatypes in Python.

Concatenation

Concatenation is when you join together two or more strings, making one single one. We can do this by using the + operator and the * operator can be used to repeat that string for a specified number of times.

```
str1 = 'Hello'

str2 ='World!'

# using +

print('str1 + str2 = ', str1 + str2)

# using *

print('str1 * 3 =', str1 * 3)
```

You can also concatenate by writing string literals together.

What if you wanted to concatenate a pair of strings that were on different lines? For this, we would use parentheses:

```
>>> # putting two string literals together

>>> 'Hello ''World!'

'Hello, World!'


>>> # by using parentheses

>>> s = ('Hello '

...      'World')

>>> s

'Hello World'
```

Iterating Through a String

Iteration through a string is possible with the for loop. Have a look at the next example, which counts how many instances of 'l' are in a string:

```
count = 0

for the letters in 'Hello World':

    if(letter == 'l'):

        count += 1

print(count,'letters found')
```

String Membership Test

Using the in keyword, we can test to see a specified substring is in a string:

```
>>> 'a' in 'program'

True

>>> 'at' not in 'battle'

False
```

Built-in functions to Work with Python

There are quite a few built-in functions that will work with string and two of the most common ones are len() and enumerate(). len() will return the number of characters, or the length of a string while enumeration() will return an enumerate object. That object will have the index and value pairs of the items in the string.

```
str = 'hot'

# enumerate()

list_enumerate = list(enumerate(str))

print('list(enumerate(str) = ', list_enumerate)

#character count

print('len(str) = ', len(str))
```

String Formatting

• Escape Sequence

If you wanted a text printed that said, 'she said, "what's that?"' we cannot use single quoted, nor can we use double quotes. Doing so would give us a SyntaxError because the text contains single and double quotes.

```
>>> print("She said, "What's that?"")

...
```

```
SyntaxError: invalid syntax

>>> print('She said, "What's that?"')

...

SyntaxError: invalid syntax
```

A way around this would be to use the triple quotes or we can use an escape sequence.

Escape sequences begin with a backslash   and they are interpreted a little differently. If single quotes are used as a string representation, then the escape sequence would have to escape all the single quotes in the string and the same thing applies to double quotes. This is how we would do that with the text from the example above:

```
# using triple quotes

print('''She said, "What's that?"''')

# escaping single quotes

print('She said, "What\'s that?"')

# escaping double quotes

print("She said, \"What's that?\"")
```

These are all of the escape sequences that Python supports:

Escape Sequence	Description
\newline	the backslash and the newline ignored
\\	backslash
\'	single quote marks
\"	double quote marks

\a	ASCII Bell
\b	ASCII Backspace
\f	ASCII Formfeed
\n	ASCII Linefeed
\r	ASCII Carriage Return
\t	ASCII Horizontal Tab
\v	ASCII Vertical Tab
\ooo	any character with the octal value of ooo
\xHH	any character with a hexadecimal value of HH

Have a look at these examples:

```
>>> print("C:\\Python32\\Lib")
C:\Python32\Lib
```

```
>>> print("This is printed\nin two lines")
This will be printed
over two lines
```

```
>>> print("This is \x48\x45\x58 representation")
This is a HEX representation
```

Raw String

Sometimes, there may be a need to ignore the escape sequence in a string. To do this, we use an r or an R at the front of the string, telling the interpreter that it is a raw string and that any escape sequence that is in the string is to be ignored.

```
>>> print("This is \x61 \nvery good example")

This is a

Very good example

>>> print(r"This is \x61 \nvery good example")

This is \x61 \nvery good example
```

Chapter 9: Python Sets

A Python set is a collection of items in no particular order. Each item in the set is unique, there are no duplicate items and the set is items or elements must be immutable, meaning they cannot be changed. That said, the actual set is mutable so you can add items to it and you can remove items from it.

We use sets to carry out mathematical set operations, such as symmetric difference, intersection, union, etc.

How to create a set

A set is created by placing all the elements inside a set of curly braces, each item separated from the next by a comma. We can also use the set() function, built into Python. You may have as many items as you want in a   set and they don't have to be of the same datatype either. However, none of the items can be mutable:

```python
# a set of integers

my_set = {4, 5, 6}

print(my_set)

# a set of mixed datatypes

my_set = {2.0, "Hello", (4, 5, 6)}

print(my_set)
```

Have a go at these examples too:

```python
# a set does not have any duplicates

# Output: {4, 5, 6, 7}

my_set = {4, 5, 6, 7, 6, 5}
```

```
print(my_set)

# a set cannot have any mutable items

# here [6, 7] is a mutable list

# If you uncommented line #12,

# this will cause this error.

# TypeError: unhashable type: 'list'

#my_set = {4, 5, [6, 7]}

# we can make a set from a list

# Output: {4, 5, 6}

my_set = set([4, 5, 6, 5])

print(my_set)
```

It isn't very easy to create a set that is empty. If you used a set of empty curly braces {} it would only create an empty dictionary. If you want to make a set that doesn't have any elements we would need to use the set() function but without using any arguments.

```
# we initialize a with {}

a = {}

# we check the data type of a

# Output: <class 'dict'>

print(type(a))

# we initialize a with a set()

a = set()

# we check the data type of a

# Output: <class 'set'>

print(type(a))
```

How to change a set in Python

While a set is mutable, the elements are not in any particular order and this means that indexing won't work. We also cannot use slicing to access or to change a set element because neither slicing nor indexing are supported by set().

What we can do is add an element to the set by using the add() method and we can add several elements by using the update() method. The update() method will take lists, tuples, strings or any other set as an argument. No matter which way it is done, there are to be no duplicates.

```python
# initialize my_set

my_set = {4, 6}

print(my_set)

# if you uncommented line 9,

# you would get an error

# TypeError: the 'set' object does not support indexing

#my_set[0]

# add an element

# Output: {4, 5, 6}

my_set.add(2)

print(my_set)

# add multiple elements

# Output: {4, 5, 6, 7}

my_set.update([5, 6, 7])

print(my_set)
```

```
# add list and set

# Output: {4, 5, 6, 7, 8, 9, 11}

my_set.update([7, 8], {4, 9, 11})

print(my_set)
```

When this program is run, the output should be:

```
{4, 6}
```

```
{4, 5, 6}
```

```
{4, 5, 6, 7}
```

```
{4, 5, 6, 7, 8, 9, 11}
```

Removing elements from a set

You can remove a specific item from a set by using the remove() and discard() methods. There is just one difference between these two methods – with discard(), if an element doesn't actually exist in set, the set will remain as it is but, with remove(), this would raise an error. Look at the next example to see how this works:

```
# initialize my_set

my_set = {4, 5, 6, 7, 8}

print(my_set)

# discard an element

# Output: {4, 5, 6, 7}

my_set.discard(4)

print(my_set)

# remove an element
```

```python
# Output: {4, 5, 7}

my_set.remove(6)

print(my_set)

# discard one element

# it is not present in my_set

# Output: {4, 5, 7}

my_set.discard(2)

print(my_set)

# remove one element

# it is not present in my_set

# If you uncommented line 27,

# you would get an error.

# Output: KeyError: 2

#my_set.remove(2)
```

In the same way, we can also use pop() method to remove and then return and item in the set.

Because the set is not in any order, we can't tell which of the items will get popped; it is pretty random.

The clear() method will let you remove all the elements form the set:

```python
# initialize my_set

# Output: a set of unique elements

my_set = set("HelloWorld")

print(my_set)
```

```python
# pop one element

# Output: random element

print(my_set.pop())

# pop another element

# Output: random element

my_set.pop()

print(my_set)

# clear my_set

#Output: set()

my_set.clear()

print(my_set)
```

Chapter 10: Python Objects and Classes

Python is object oriented and this means that all the focus of the language is on objects and not on anything else. An object is nothing more than a collection of variables and functions – the functions act on the variables. A class is a blueprint of the object. We can create several objects from one class and each object is called the instance of the class. To create this object, we use a process known as instantiation.

Defining a Class

Like the function definition starts with the def keyword, the class definition begins with the class keyword. The first string is known as the docstring and it briefly describes the class and what is does. You do not need to include this but it is recommended. Have a look at this class definition

```
class MyNewClass:

    '''This is a docstring. A new class has been created'''

    pass
```

classes create new local namespaces and these are where all the class attributes get defined. The attributes may be functions or they may be data. There are also a few special attributes and each begins with a double underscore. For example, to get the docstring of the class, we would use __doc__.

The minute a class is defined, a new class object will be created and it will have the same name. It is his object that gives us access to all the attributes and it lets us instantiate any new object of the class.   Try this next example:

```python
class MyClass:
    "This is the second class"
    a = 10
    def func(self):
        print('Hello')
# Output: 10
print(MyClass.a)
# Output: <function MyClass.func at 0x0000000003079BF8>
print(MyClass.func)
# Output: 'This is my second class'
print(MyClass.__doc__)
```

Run this program and you should see this as the output:

```
10
<function 0x7feaa932eae8="" at="" myclass.func="">
This is the second class
```

Creating an Object

The class object gives us access to the attributes and it allows for instantiation of new class objects. The process we use of this is much like the process used for a function call:

```python
>>> ob = MyClass()
```

This creates a new instance object with a name of ob. Now we can gain access to the object attributes by using the name prefix. The attributes could be methods or they could be data. An object method is a function that corresponds to that class. A function method that is also a class attribute will define a new method for the objects of the class. By this, we mean that, because MyClass.func is an attribute of the class or a function object, ob.func will then be a method object:

```python
class MyClass:

    "This is the second class"

    a = 10

    def func(self):

        print('Hello')
# create a new MyClass

ob = MyClass()

# Output: <function MyClass.func at 0x000000000335B0D0>

print(MyClass.func)

#     Output:     <bound     method     MyClass.func     of
<__main__.MyClass object at 0x000000000332DEF0>>

print(ob.func)

# Calling function func()

# Output: Hello

ob.func()
```

You may have seen that we put the self-parameter in the function definition in the class but the method was called as ob.func() without any parameters or arguments – but it worked. The reason for this is that when an object calls its own methods, the object will be passed as the initial argument so ob.func() becomes MyClass.func(ob).

Generally, when you call a method with n number of arguments, it is the same as calling the function with a list of arguments created by putting the object of the method before the argument. It is because of this that the first argument of the class function should be the object and this is called self.

Constructors

When a class function starts with a double underscore, it is a special function that has a special meaning. The __init__ function is one of the more interesting because it is called whenever a new class object gets instantiated. These functions are also known as constructors in Python and in any other Object-Oriented Programming language.

Of one particular interest is the __init__() function. This special function gets called whenever a new object of that class is instantiated. They are used to initialize the variables:

```python
class ComplexNumber:

    def __init__(self,r = 0,i = 0):

        self.real = r

        self.imag = i

    def getData(self):

        print("{0}+{1}j".format(self.real,self.imag))

# Create a new ComplexNumber object

c1 = ComplexNumber(2,3)

# Call getData() function

# Output: 2+3j

c1.getData()

# Create another ComplexNumber object

# and create a new attribute 'attr'

c2 = ComplexNumber(5)

c2.attr = 10
```

```
# Output: (5, 0, 10)

print((c2.real, c2.imag, c2.attr))

# but c1 object doesn't have attribute 'attr'

#  AttributeError:  'ComplexNumber'  object  has  no
attribute 'attr'

c1.attr
```

In this example, we have defined a new class that represents complex numbers. There are two functions in the class; __init__, which initializes the variables and getData() which properly displays the number. One interesting note is that object attributes can be created as you go. In the above example, a new attribute, called attr, was created for object c2 and it was read as well.

Deleting Attributes and Objects

Any object attribute may be deleted at any time and we do this by using the statement called del. Have a go at the following on your interpreter:

```
>>> c1 = ComplexNumber(2,3)

>>> del c1.imag

>>> c1.getData()

Traceback (most recent call last):

...

AttributeError: 'ComplexNumber' object has no attribute 'imag'

>>> del ComplexNumber.getData

>>> c1.getData()
```

```
Traceback (most recent call last):

...

AttributeError: 'ComplexNumber' object has no attribute
'getData'
```

You can also use the del statement to delete the actual object.

```
>>> c1 = ComplexNumber(1,3)

>>> del c1

>>> c1

Traceback (most recent call last):

...

NameError: name 'c1' is not defined
```

It is a little more complicated than that. When c1 = ComplexNumber(1, 3) is done, a brand-new instance object gets created in memory and it is bound with c1. When the command, del c1, is given, the binding gets removed and the c1 name gets deleted from the namespace that corresponds to it. However, the object stays in memory and, provided another name doesn't bind to it, it will later be destroyed automatically. This is known a garbage collection.

Chapter 11: Python Dictionary

A dictionary is a collection of unordered items. While some of the compound datatypes have just a value as an element, the dictionary has a key, value pair. A dictionary is fully optimized to get a value but only when the key is known

Creating a Dictionary

This is very simple; all we do is put the elements of the dictionary inside a set of curly braces, with each element separated by a comma. Each item has a key and a value and these are expressed as the key:value pair.   The values may be of any datatype and they can repeat themselves but they must be immutable and they must be unique.

An element has a key and the corresponding value expressed as a pair, key: value.

```
# an empty dictionary

my_dict = {}

# a dictionary with integer keys

my_dict = {1: 'apple', 2: 'ball'}

# a dictionary with mixed keys

my_dict = {'name': 'John', 1: [2, 4, 3]}

# using dict()

my_dict = dict({1:'apple', 2:'ball'})

# from a sequence having each item as a pair

my_dict = dict([(1,'apple'), (2,'ball')])
```

As you can see from this example, we can also use the built-in function called dict() to create a dictionary.

Accessing Dictionary Elements

While we can use indexing with some types to gain access to the values, in the dictionary we use keys. These keys may be inside a set of square brackets or they may be accessed using the get() method.   The difference is, with the get() method, the result returned will be None whereas with the other method, if a key is not found we would get the KeyError.

```
my_dict = {'name':'Jake', 'age': 27}

# Output: Jake

print(my_dict['name'])

# Output: 27

print(my_dict.get('age'))

# Trying to access keys which don't exist will give us
an error

# my_dict.get('address')

# my_dict['address']
```

The output of this will be:

```
Jake

27
```

Changing or Adding Elements to a Dictionary

A dictionary is mutable so we can add items and we can change the values of existing ones by using the assignment operator. If the key is already there, the value will be updated but, if it isn't, a new key:value pair will be added.

```python
my_dict = {'name':'Jake', 'age': 26}

# update value

my_dict['age'] = 27

#Output: {'age': 27, 'name': 'Jake'}

print(my_dict)

# add item

my_dict['address'] = 'Uptown'

# Output: {'address': 'Uptown', 'age': 27, 'name': 'Jake'}

print(my_dict)
```

the output of this will be:

```python
{'name': 'Jake', 'age': 27}

{'name': 'Jake', 'age': 27, 'address': 'Uptown'}
```

Deleting or Removing Dictionary Elements

Specific items can be removed form a dictionary with the pop() method. This method will remove the item using the key provided and will then return the value. popitem() will remove an arbitrary item and return it from the dictionary or, if you want to remove all items at one, you can use the clear() method.

The keyword del can be used to remove specified individual items or the entire dictionary.

```python
# remove an arbitrary element

# Output: (1, 1)

print(squares.popitem())

# Output: {2: 4, 3: 9, 5: 25}
```

```python
print(squares)

# delete a specified element

del squares[5]

# Output: {2: 4, 3: 9}

print(squares)

# remove all the elements

squares.clear()

# Output: {}

print(squares)

# delete the entire dictionary

del squares

# Throws an Error

# print(squares)
```

The output of this will be:

```
16

{1: 1, 2: 4, 3: 9, 5: 25}

(1, 1)

{2: 4, 3: 9, 5: 25}

{2: 4, 3: 9}

{}
```

There are several methods that will work with dictionary and you have seen some of the already:

In all the following, d will default to None

Method	Description
clear()	will remove all the items out of the dictionary
copy()	will return a shallow copy of the specified dictionary
fromkeys(seq[, v])	will return a new dictionary containing keys equal to v from both seq and value
get(key[, d])	will return the key value If there is no key, it will return d
items()	will return a new view of the key:value pair in the dictionary
keys()	will return a new view of the keys
pop(key[, d])	will remove the element with the key and will return the value or will return d if the key isn't found. If the key isn't found and d isn't given, we get a KeyError
popitem()	will remove an arbitrary key o value and return it. If the dictionary is empty, a KeyError is raised
setdefault(key[, d])	if the key is present in the dictionary, the value will be returned. If it isn't, the key will be inserted with the value d and d will be returned

These are some examples of how these methods are used:

```python
marks = {}.fromkeys(['Biology','Math','Physics'], 0)

# Output: {'Math': 0, 'Biology': 0, 'Physics': 0}

print(marks)

for item in marks.items():

    print(item)

# Output: ['Math', 'Biology', 'Physics']

list(sorted(marks.keys()))
```

Dictionary Comprehension

Dictionary comprehension is similar to list comprehension and is a nice way of creating a new dictionary from a Python iterable. It is made up of an expression key:value pair and the a for statement which is inside a set of curly braces. This is an example of creating a dictionary using elements, which are a pair of a number and its corresponding square.

```python
squares = {x: x*x for x in range(6)}

# Output: {0: 0, 1: 1, 2: 4, 3: 9, 4: 16, 5: 25}

print(squares)

This code is equivalent to

squares = {}

for x in range(6):

    squares[x] = x*x
```

Dictionary comprehensions can have as many for statements or if statements as you want. If statements are used to filter the items out and to create the new dictionary. These are a few examples of how to create a dictionary with just odd elements.

```python
odd_squares = {x: x*x for x in range(11) if x%2 == 1}

# Output: {1: 1, 3: 9, 5: 25, 7: 49, 9: 81}
```

```
print(odd_squares)
```

Other Dictionary Operations

• Membership Test

Dictionaries can be tested to see if a key is present and we do that with the in keyword. Membership tests are only for keys, never for values.

```
squares = {1: 1, 3: 9, 5: 25, 7: 49, 9: 81}

# Output: True

print(1 in squares)

# Output: True

print(2 not in squares)

# membership tests for key only not value

# Output: False

print(49 in squares)
```

Iterating Through Dictionary

A for loop will allow you to iterate through the keys in a dictionary:

```
squares = {1: 1, 3: 9, 5: 25, 7: 49, 9: 81}

for i in squares:

    print(squares[i])
```

Built-in Functions

There are a number of built-in functions that can be used with dictionary, each for a different task:

Function	Description
all()	will return True only if all the dictionary keys are true or if it is an empty dictionary
any()	will return True if one or more keys are true while if it is an empty dictionary, False will be returned
len()	will return the length of the dictionary
cmp()	Will compare the elements in two dictionaries
sorted()	Will return a new list of sorted keys within the dictionary

These are a few examples of how the built-in functions work:

```
squares = {1: 1, 3: 9, 5: 25, 7: 49, 9: 81}

# Output: 5

print(len(squares))

# Output: [1, 3, 5, 7, 9]

print(sorted(squares))
```

Chapter 12: Python Glossary

To finish, these are the most common terms you will come across as you learn Python:

- ">>>" – the default shell prompt in Python
- abs – will return the absolute value of any number
- argument – information used by the computer to perform the commands
- argparse – a parser that is used for command-line operations, subcommands and arguments
- assert – used while debugging to look for any conditions that should apply
- assignment – the act of giving a variable a value
- block – piece of code grouped together
- break – used to break out of a for loop or out of a while loop
- class – a blueprint or template by which objects are defined
- compiler – the program that translates your code from a high-level to a low-level language
- continue – skips the current block and returns to the while or for statement
- conditional statement – a statement that has an if statement or an if...else statement
- debugging – a process by which program errors are found and removed
- def – the keyword that defines a method or function
- dictionary – a mutable array of key:value pairs

- distutils – a package already in the Standard Library and used for installing, building and distributing the code
- docstring – a string literal that is the first statement inside a module, class, method or function definition
- __future__ - a pseudo-module used by programmers to enable features in the language that are not compatible with the interpreter
- easy_install – a Python module that is included with setuptools and allows for automatic downloading, building, installing and management of Python packages
- evaluation order – the order in which expressions and assignments are evaluated – expressions are evaluated left to right but assignments are evaluated right-hand side before the left
- exceptions – breaking out of a code block's flow control to handle exceptions or errors
- expression – a piece of code that produces some value
- filter – a filter, (function, Sequence) will return a sequence of items for which the function evaluates true
- float – a floating point number that is immutable
- for -   a loop that will iterate over an object that can be iterated over, capturing the local variable elements for the attached block to use
- function – a sequence of events with parameters
- function call – invoking the function and its arguments
- garbage collection – removing anything not required and freeing up memory
- generators – functions that return iterators

- High-level language – an easy language for humans to read and write
- IDLE – the Integrated Development Environment
- if statement – executes a code block dependent on conditions. Also includes else and elif
- immutable – not able to be changed once created and/or assigned
- import – for importing modules that contain variables or functions that may be used in the current program
- indentation – used to delimit blocks and identify statements
- int – an integer that is immutable
- interactive mode – interpreter is interactive when it reads commands from a tty
- interpret – the execution of a program one line at a time
- IPython – the interactive Python shell
- Iterable – an object that can return its members individually
- Lambda – shorthand for creating functions that are anonymous
- List – a mutable sequence that may contain mixed datatypes
- list comprehension – a nice way of processing part of or all of the elements and returning a list of results
- literals – notations for the constant values of a few built-in datatypes
- map – (function, iterable, ...) – applies a function to each element of an iterable and returns a list of results

- methods – similar to a function but running on objects
- module – a unit of code that is imported by another code
- object – data that has value or attributes and methods
- object-oriented – lets a user manipulate the data structures to build programs and execute them
- pass – required to build empty code blocks
- PEP 8 – official recommendations for writing code in Python
- Python Package Index – the official repository for third-party Python software
- Pythonic – code or an idea which follows very closes the idioms of Python instead of using concepts that are common in other languages
- reduce (function, sequence) will return a value that is constructed when the binary function is called on the first two sequence elements, then the result and then the next element, etc.
- set – a set of elements in no particular order and with no duplicates
- Setuptools – a collection of tools that enhance Python distutils, for better building and distribution of Python packages
- slice – a sub-part of a sequence
- str – a string of characters, immutable
- strings – may include letters, numbers and other symbols, enclosed in single or double quotes – usually single quotes
- statement – part of a block of code
- try – will allow exceptions that are raised in the code block attached to be caught and then handled by an except clause

- tuple – immutable sequence that may contain mixed datatypes
- variables – containers that hold text and numbers
- = - the assignment operator, used for assigning a value to a variable
- while – will execute a code block so long as the test condition is true
- with – used in context managers to enclose code blocks
- yield – returns values from generator functions

Conclusion

At first glance, Python might seem like a complicated language to learn but once you get into it, you can see that, really, it is quite easy. It isn't something you are going to pick up on the first go around and it will take plenty of practice but, once you have grasped the basics in this book, you can move on to more complicated concepts and learn how to become an expert programmer.

As I said right at the start, Python has a very active community and you really should make use of this. Join the forums, join in with the conversations and offer help where you can; the community will be only too happy to put you right when you find yourself struggling.

There are also plenty of online courses you can take, some free, some paid, and a whole wealth of Python programming information and documentation that you can turn to.

Good luck in your bid to become a Python programmer; the most important thing to remember, above all, is to have fun!

References

https://docs.python.org

www.programiz.com

Other Books By iCode Academy

If you want to know more about other books from the series, click on the link in each title:

Book 1 : **Python Programming: Your Step by Step Guide to Easily Learn Python in 7 Days**

Book 2 : Programming For Beginners: 3 Manuscripts in 1 Bundle - Python For Beginners, Java Programming and Html & CSS For Beginners

Book 3: **HTML & CSS For Beginners: Your Step by Step Guide to Easily HtmL & Css Programming in 7 Days**

Book 4: C Programming for Beginners: Your Guide to Easily Learn C Programming In 7 Days

Book 5: JQuery For Beginners: Your Guide To Easily Learn jQuery Programming in 7 Days

Book 6: HTML5 and CSS3 for Beginners: Your Guide To Easily Learn Html5 and Css3 in 7 Days

Book 7: Ruby For Beginners: Your Guide To Easily Learn Ruby in 7 Days

Did you enjoy this book?

I want to thank you for purchasing and reading this book. I really hope you got a lot out of it.

Can I ask a quick favor though?

If you enjoyed this book I would really appreciate it if you could leave me a positive review on Amazon.

I love getting feedback from my customers and reviews on Amazon really do make a difference. We read all our reviews and would really appreciate your thoughts.

Thanks so much.

iCode Academy

p.s. You can click here to go directly to the book on Amazon and leave your review.

Made in the USA
Monee, IL
07 July 2026

56551625R00066